Pilgrims *of the* Infinite

A book of insights

Manoj Pavithran

First Published in 2020

Becomeshakespeare.com
One Point Six Technologies Pvt. Ltd.
119-123, 1st Floor, Building J2, B - Wing,
Wadala Truck Terminal, Wadala East,
Mumbai 400022, Maharashtra, INDIA
T: +91 8080226699

Cover photo by Bishnu Bidari from Pixabay

ISBN - 978-93-90463-18-3

Disclaimer

This is not a guidebook for spiritual practitioners
but a sharing of my personal journey.

Dedication

To

Sri Aurobindo and The Mother

Acknowledgements

I am grateful to Divyanshi Chugh for her loving insistence and continuous support in publishing this book. Without her support, this book wouldn't have happened. She has not only helped me to compile and organise the contents from my Facebook posts but also found the right publisher! Thank you Divyanshi for your loving presence in my life.

I am grateful to Mini Hariharan who, many years ago, first suggested the idea of compiling my Facebook posts and publishing it as a book. She even did the first compilation. Thank you, Mini for planting the idea and getting it moving.

I am grateful to Gayatri Majumdar who initially edited some chapters of the book and gave very useful feedback.

I am grateful to Dr Devdas Menon for writing the forward for this book; he is someone whom I admire quietly and had the privilege of working with.

I must acknowledge all my friends on Facebook who with their comments and appreciation gently nudged me to become a writer.

I am grateful to my parents for giving me a beautiful experience of growing up as their son in the bounty of Nature amidst coconut trees, paddy fields, ponds and backwaters of Kerala. It has deeply moulded my perceptions.

I am grateful to my publisher and their professional team for materialising and distributing this book.

Thank you all for giving me birth and all your loving support.

I feel like I am still discovering the writer in me.

Preface

There is a process of spiritual awakening, a process that unfolds naturally like the growth and flowering of a tree. By spiritual awakening, I do not mean anything spectacular or dramatic. In fact, when I started suspecting that there is a spiritual process unfolding and learned about the possibility of enlightenment I was expecting some spectacular results of enlightenment. Decades went by without anything miraculous and dramatic happening and all that I noticed was a growing sense of peace and settled calm. It took me years to give up the idea of enlightenment and start loving life as it is and surrender to the sculpting hands of the infinite. Then it became much simpler to be a nobody in particular and accept my ignorance and start walking the path like a pilgrim.

Life has become much simpler, the sun is rising as usual and probably the only difference is I am experiencing life more vividly and fluidly than ever before with greater creative richness. Also, I have become much less embarrassed to talk about God or the Divine. There are fewer fears, and more hopes and dreams. Life is beautiful and there is so much to learn. The Master has kept the masterplan a secret and that adds to the mystery.

I see a world in transition, a grand process of transformation of human nature is unfolding and more and more people are drawn into its call. Those who are clueless are frightened and those who are open are gladly surrendering to the process.

I am a traveller on the way, a pilgrim of the infinite. These insights and observations are to share my journey with you hoping that this may be of value to some of you.

With gratitude to the one who is gazing through you.

We are two sides of the same being.

This book is an invitation and an offering.

Manoj Pavithran
Auroville
1 October 2020

Foreword

This book "Pilgrims of the Infinite" is a set of powerful inspirations that come to us providentially through the agency of Manoj Pavithran. They are a collection of free-flowing words — cast in the form of single sentences, poems and poetic prose – snippets that Manoj has been sharing with friends through Facebook posts, over the past many years. He has thoughtfully assembled them, for our benefit, in the form of eight chapters, each with a theme having contents that flow naturally into the next theme – starting with Solitude and Silence, and ending with Love and Purpose.

There is a mantra-like quality in the writing – as though the words emerge from a wordless Consciousness that is higher, wider, deeper and richer than what our minds can access. It is this mantric quality that makes this book special. Reading any verse or paragraph on any page at random is bound to reveal this to any sensitive soul. The words are in simple English; it is a simplicity that expresses all that is true, good and beautiful.

This is truly a book of insights that is bound to resonate with any sincere spiritual aspirant, and especially one who seeks to understand the teachings of Sri Aurobindo, who is the guiding spirit of the author of this book. It is an experiential sharing of a spiritual journey full of trials and tribulations, and ups and downs, blooming into a mature and reverential recognition of the guiding Presence of the divine in one's innermost being. Nowhere in the writing is there any trace of pride of accomplishment; there is only a continual learning, loving, surrendering and revelling in the delight of divine grace.

I am grateful to Manoj for his kind invitation to me to write this Foreword. He has been a wonderful support, during the past decade, for our courses for students at IIT Madras on Self Awareness and Integral Karmayoga, as well as our annual workshops for teachers from all over the country. He transmits a spontaneous, kind and still Presence to all who take part in his gatherings.

Thank you, Manoj, for being who you are, and for your generous sharing!

Without further ado, may I suggest, dear reader, that you plunge straight into the contents of this book and taste the nectar it offers. Pause every now and then, to contemplate - on whatever appeals to you, or even if it meets with some inner resistance. May you relish and internalise these insights, and abide in the Silence underlying the words!

Devdas Menon

About the Author

Manoj, who grew up in Kerala, is an explorer of Integral Yoga Psychology and its transformational practice for the evolution of consciousness. He started exploring Integral Yoga in 1989 right after graduating as a production engineer. He did post-graduate studies in Product Design from the National Institute of Design (NID), Ahmedabad, India in 1993. After a short period of working as a professional design consultant, he quit the profession and joined Auroville in 1995 to immerse in Integral Yoga and collective evolution.

Currently, he is a member of Auroville Campus Initiative (https://aci.auroville.org/) where he is actively involved in re-imagining higher education based on the principles of integral education. He has co-founded Telos (www.telos.org.in) focusing on the practical applications of Integral Yoga Psychology. He makes 3D motion graphics videos to share the vision and work of Sri Aurobindo (www.sopanam.org). He has also created Auronet, the intranet portal of Auroville and is involved in its software development and loves information technology and its role in building communities, collective self-awareness, and creativity.

This is his first book.

Prologue

He who chooses the Infinite has been chosen by the Infinite.

- Sri Aurobindo

Contents

Chapter 1

Solitude

When pain takes you home, go alone.

~

Those who have the call will know it in their solitude.

~

If you have not listened to your own heart,
How can you ever listen to others?

~

Cherishing solitude is a sign that
You have found something precious within you.

~

When love demands your solitude,
Bear the tides all alone;
A greater love demands
A wider shore.

~

When you are all alone in a crowd
And a living presence envelops
Your thoughts with a whisper
Of a love that has no name
Behold the one behind the multitude
And be still for the doors to open.

~

When you are alone,
Trust the solitude
Trust the winds
And the whispers.

Listen deep
As if someone dear
Is near, hiding
In your own depths
Waiting as if
You are coming home.

~

However sweet an attachment is, it still binds you.
To enjoy the flight of an eagle, you must leave
Leave behind the warmth of your nest.

In your solitude are the heights,
In your solitude are the wings always wide,
In your solitude are the winds of life beneath your wings.

In the blue infinite is your vast horizon.
Therein lies the freedom
That has no demands upon your time.
You are the space, all containing space.
Time is yet to be born.

In your perfect stillness, the wings of reason come to rest;
In your silent gaze the heart knows its melody;
Upon your trails, the fire is born ever new.

In you are the time born, in you are the colours of light,
In you are the unknown songs.
When your seeing is free, time opens her secrets.
When your hearing is wide, space unfolds her mystery.
Where they intersect, you are born free.

When you are self-born you are always fresh,
As if the sun-kissed earth has found her beloved;
Then your body of the earth is married to the sun.

~

All tools and techniques have a place;
They can give you a good start
But as you dive deeper all techniques fail inevitably.
In fact, even the knowledge that took you there fails;
That is even more disturbing than the tools that have failed.

There is a no man's land of the void
Where you have nothing but your lonely self to settle with,
An empty cup that is yet to be filled
With the fresh breath of Spirit.
Our instinct is to rush back to the pile of knowledge
Or to cling to people who are dear and near
In a vain attempt to fill the mind and heart.

But once the call is upon you nothing will satisfy,
In fact, everything falls apart meaningless
Leaving you alone to deal with your solitude.
Slowly you discover that you are longing for another shore,
For another kind of sweetness.
Then experience seeps in gently like a cool breeze.
It gives you a joy that is complete in itself
Making everything else graceful in its presence.

Then it withdraws leaving you behind
In the void, empty and meaningless.
It won't come back in spite of all your tools and
techniques.
And then you learn to wait,
Wait for a long time
Patiently even when there is no result;
But with a prayer in your heart.

~

"You mean you sit alone in that empty railway station?" I asked with astonishment.

"Yes, I do it often," he said with a mysterious smile.

It was long ago, somewhere in 1986 or 87, when I was in the process of turning inward and this conversation was one of the decisive moments. I was talking to a dear friend in college, someone who was a loner by nature with whom I had a special bond. We did not meet regularly but when we met, often we had interesting conversations. It was during one such conversation he revealed this as if sharing a very private secret.

There was a small meter-gauge railway station right next to our college and most of the time the station remained empty as the trains were very rare on that route. So my friend found it to be an ideal place to go and sit alone and explore his solitude.

Till then the very idea of sitting alone never crossed my mind as an interesting thing to do. Like everyone else, I sought the company of my friends to spend my time with and the group dynamics was the source of my identity. But that conversation changed it forever. It was time to leave behind the group identity and mass consciousness; it was time to become an individual.

Suddenly I found myself getting drawn to a mystery and I knew there is something in it that I must explore. I did not ask him what exactly he did sitting alone in that railway station as somehow I knew that the very act of sitting alone is an adventure. The very idea of leaving behind all friends to chart a course where you are utterly alone had a magnetic pull. It was challenging and I was ready.

The conversation happened to be a trigger that woke up the call for solitude. Now when I look back, I understand the process of individualisation but while passing through it, I had no idea what I was into.

Soon I found myself sitting alone in that railway station trying to figure out what it meant to be in solitude. Later I found an interesting corner in the college where I could sit alone without getting disturbed by anyone. But without having anything to do, my mind was wondering what to do. Then I found a way to gather my mind. It was a simple ritual of sculpting on pieces of white chalk. I used to collect the leftover pieces from the classroom and using a fine carving tool, I made them into miniature sculptures. It was an act in which I could forget about the world and about myself; there was only this highly concentrated act of sculpting that revealed interesting forms. I didn't even know that it was an active form of concentrated meditation.

When you are consciously absorbed in an action in which you no more remember the passing of time or the world around you or even about yourself, there, in that space, the awakening rays find their way to lead you home where the rays are born out of pure delight.

~

When you are left alone
When you have nothing particular to do
Other than watching the doer,
Wonder at the mind building up thoughts
Wonder at life reaching out to act
Wonder at the body engaging in work all on its own
Carried by life's response to the mind,
Wonder at what you are in all this.

Sitting alone under the moonshine
Watching the silhouettes of tall trees
Immersing in the sound of stillness
A quiet gladness wells up
A smile for no reason
A joy that is complete
A love that has no bounds
And you wonder how wholesome it is.

As you feel your feet doing the walk
As you feel your hands washing a fruit
As you behold the water dear
As you enjoy a shower
And immersed in all that is
Being whole and complete
You smile at the mind building up thoughts
And wonder why the mind is so busy
With its own world when
The shower of Grace is already present.

My dear mind, I would like you to let go
Of all your plans, of all your dreams
Of all your worries and your will to be.
And just be the ocean and enjoy
The winds rolling out your waves
The stars guarding your secrets
The dawn's infinite splendours
And be still with reverence.

~

When you are all alone beneath the stars,
When you are the warm density of the earth,
When you are the mountain stillness,
Then, then alone you are ready to receive.

When you are the silence,
When you are the stillness,
When you are the depth infinite,
Then, then alone you are ready to receive.

It is not your word that speaks through you,
It is not your songs that sing through you,
It is not your call that calls through you,
It is the earth, the soul of the earth.

~

When you spend time just with yourself
And go deep within, you can find deeper streams
Of self-existent love and joy and get nourished by their
currents.
Then this stream fills your life and nurtures you.
Coming in touch with this Presence, is your way out of
loneliness.

~

Chapter 2

Silence

Who am I?

Silence, please.

~

Depth demands silence and stillness.

~

Waiting in silence is an art.

~

Keeping silence helps me to listen to other people, but the main advantage is in listening to my own depths.

~

Thoughts become friends
When we look at them as friends
And listen deeply;
Then you may find yourself
Sitting in silence.

~

You must question all things if you want to be a thinker.
But if you want to be a seer, then all questions must end in
deep silence; then the inner vision opens.

~

When you are the silence,
Truth reveals itself
And gladness deepens.

~

Silence and peace do not come by effort,
They come infusing, permeating our whole being
Like the fragrance of a flower when we relax
And open to the universe.

~

When you are curious, fascinated and intensely attentive, all questions vanish from the mind and the mind falls silent naturally. What is left is the pure joy of discovery, without having to ask questions.

~

Sometimes amidst the whirling currents of life, a ray of light finds its way all the way down to the very substance of your body. Then there is a silence, stillness and deep peace in the body that brings a deep calm breath regardless of all activities that are going on as usual.

Then, it is alright even if I do not understand a thing about life.

~

As the silence deepens, the need for conversations recedes and you settle into an ocean of energy, an energy that is always alive and present. It is a space where you sit alone and listen, listen deeply as you do not understand the language of the ocean of which you are only a tiny drop.

~

Silence is eloquent
When love speaks.

~

If you have not found
The quiet prayer in your heart
Be alone in silence
Till you feel the whisper.

~

To feel at home in your silence
To feel at home in your aloneness
To feel at home in your restfulness
To feel at home in your causeless gladness
Is to come home and wait for the door to open.

~

Not knowing no more feels strange
Waiting silence listens far and wide
Slow and steady the breath deepens
Lingers within a memory sweet
The fragrance of an invisible rose.

~

Experience walks in unarmed
A stranger whom I have always loved
Ideas deaf forgets to quarrel
Silence holds the breath in stillness
Infinite moment's eternal charm
Leaves no strings untouched
And my soul trembles naked.

~

When you are all alone beneath the stars,
When you are the warm density of the earth,
When you are the mountain stillness,
Then, then alone you are ready to receive.

When you are the silence,
When you are the stillness,
When you are the depth infinite,
Then, then alone you are ready to receive.

It is not your word that speaks through you,
It is not your songs that sing through you,
It is not your call that calls through you,
It is the earth, the memory of the earth.

~

"There is no story without surprise!" said the Rishi Parashara looking at young Vyasa, his son.

They were meeting after seven winters on the banks of Yamuna.

"I am not afraid," said Vyasa after a long silence.

"…but it overwhelms me, this ocean I have found within me".

He sat firmly with his spine straight and legs crossed, as always, with his eyes open without blinking as if seeing across time.

Parashara gazed at him for a long time as if looking into the future of Vyasa, the one who was destined to leave his measure upon the waters of Bharata. Then he said,

"Yes I know, that is why it was hidden from your own gaze. But now you are ready to face it".

"I have lost my calm, the winds are upon me, the tides are overwhelming me, the seasons are furious and the elements raging".

"They were always there my son, you knew not their world or their language".

Vyasa closed his eyes and asked his father,

"How am I to contain them within me, I am losing myself".

Parashara smiled and said, "Yes, it is time to lose yourself…"

Open your eyes, see the stars above, they are your guardians…".

Vyasa opened his eyes; he saw the sky full of stars.

"To contain the ocean within you, be wide as the sky".

Parashara spoke as if the sky spoke through him. He continued,

"Forget about yourself, when you are not there the stars will speak to the ocean and the tides shall subside, the seasons shall harmonise and the elements dance".

Vyasa leaned against a rock and gazed far and wide.

There was only stillness and silence.

There was nothing more to be said.

~

Whenever there is a disturbance, whether it is an emotional disturbance or a cloud of confusion in the mind, I find it most effective to turn inward into the inner silence and quietude so that peace can come in and settle for the clouds to clear and clarity to arise. Trying to understand or solve it by an active effort usually brings more murkiness and confusion. Opening to silence and peace is an all-purpose remedy to solve most of the difficulties. Then something greater than our little self can enter and embrace us with its infinite love and wisdom along with its peace, clarity, and the lightness of being.

~

I was happy to visit my family temple in the morning. The temple is close to backwaters and the visit to the temple is also an opportunity to be near this flowing water, a stream that is always different and yet looks the same regardless of decades gone.

On one side my mind comes up with its curiosity to find out what these gods and goddesses in our temple mean, but then when I shift out of my thinking mind into to the eternity of this moment everything comes alive, without words, a living presence, ancient as this river and yet living and inviting to drop all that my mind knows and enter the silence…

To know is not necessarily to think.

Another world awaits where thoughts end.

~

I was invited for tea with my Japanese friend and it is always my pleasure to be with him. His Japanese way of drinking tea in silence is always a special moment in time. Though I have been enjoying tea with him for some time now, it is always something special the more I enter the experience through the door of silence.

When the silence deepens and the experience gets free from the veil of words, what is left is the living moment of eternity, fresh as always. The taste that has no name, the sounds that are just pure sounds, the fragrance, the movements of the body, occasional thoughts passing by, the winds, the chime… there is stillness and the pure taste of existence. There is no haste, nowhere to go, nothing to accomplish, nothing to speak, just be the taste, the sounds, the living moment.

A drop of the fresh moment is enough to rejuvenate your whole being.

It is a great way to explore how the tea reveals many messages on each stage of brewing. First time when you brew, the tea is in shock, meeting the hot water suddenly after a long period of sleep, especially as it was today, the 45-year-old Oolong tea. So you get some mild bitter taste, just waking up. When you brew it again, the tea begins to relax and starts revealing older memories and the taste changes. Every time when you brew the same leaves, you get deeper into the experience of the tea plant that has grown up somewhere and gone through many experiences until it has reached you. It is as if you are meeting someone, a being, who has a story to tell you. Then drinking tea becomes magical. It helps when you remain silent, not only physically but also mentally, without any mental chatter. Then you can focus on the experience and through the water in which the tea has released the memories, you can get an imprint in your consciousness. The more you are silent and receptive, the more you experience the tea as the tea experiences itself.

~

The mind will ask questions; it is in the nature of the mind and the mind develops by learning to ask the right questions. With every insight, clarity and joy increases. But if you want to go beyond the mind, you must renounce all your questions and the use of verbal language as a means to know.

To learn the language of the soul, mental silence is an essential condition. This does not mean the death of the mind, as the mind becomes increasingly silent and passive, something beyond the mind starts expressing itself through the mind. The mind becomes a means to receive and transmit, not a means to struggle with its questions. There is a non-linear and spontaneous way of knowing, a far more delightful and lucid way...

~

"Answers are like prisons, why do you want that?" asked the old man, he was not joking, I could see that in his eyes. He did that often, refusing to give me answers and keep the mystery alive.

As a child, radio was a great mystery to me; I used to imagine small people inside a radio and I would imagine them talking and that was the only rational possibility I could think of for radio to work. Later I learned about electronics and wave transmissions and the whole lot of explanations that took away the mystery.

Now I know the answers and with it ended the sense of wonder in life. That is the trouble with answers; they give you a blanket over the mysteries of life. We believe that we know how a seed sprouts or how our nails grow and this belief takes away all our curiosity. With that, the doors to magic were shut.

He was my ideal, the wise old man who I thought knew everything. With him time was luxurious, he gazed at plants as if he had never seen them before, he could look at the same plant, again and again, every day and I used to get impatient while going out for a walk with him. There was nothing special about most plants and yet he could just stand and gaze at them.

Once someone asked him "What is God?" and I was a bit shocked when he said, "It is a word". When he answered questions, he stripped away all the answers we already knew and put us back into the world of facts. There I was facing the fact that God is just another word, a good starting point for investigation. Then the word itself became a mystery.

When I walked out of all answers and embraced the silence in which explanations had no place, I found the window through which I can gaze at a plant without questions. Then I saw that I hardly knew anything, the mystery of life was everywhere.

We are always moving and when there is no movement, we feel restless and impatient. That is natural as we have this deep drive towards creative flowering. But the trouble of modern life is in our inability to rest and be at peace with oneself in all this movement. The idea of rest and peace is equated with being motionless, being still and it is idolised in the image of Buddha seated in lotus posture in deep meditation, stillness and peace that has moved the world in the past and still moving it in the present.

By resting or being at peace, I do not mean sitting still and motionless; the stillness of being can be retained in movement as well; resting in action is an art form we are yet to master. When the movement is upon the foundation of stillness of our being, we are at once resting and acting, we are the peace in action, dynamic peace, dynamic stillness, and dynamic silence.

It is not that thoughts shouldn't move, emotions shouldn't move, or the body and its limbs shouldn't move; all can move upon the foundation of calm inner silence and peace and move together in harmony and not pull in many directions.

When our body, its dynamic energy and manifold movements of the mind are all moving in unison obeying the inner radiance and joy upon the foundation of peace and stillness, we have the wholesome movement – without any internal conflicts, the wholesome movement of the whole, the ocean moving as a drop.

~

It is by allowing strength to arise, you gather strength in you; not by any struggle or strain of will. Strength naturally arises from within when all efforts and struggles are replaced by calm luminous clarity in the silence of your being.

~

Chapter 3

Fire

The fire that burns you also transforms you.

~

If you are afraid of your own passion,
How would you ever get to know the fire that you are?

~

To set ablaze your fire, let it consume you first.
Burn in its mighty transfiguring touch
And die in its unbearable strength;
Then you may be recast, fire-born
Poured into a new mould you have never dreamt of.

~

When the fire calls, a seeker must go
Leaving behind all that is dear.
Even when it tears him apart,
Even when it bleeds and shatters his life,
He must go in search of the fire.

That is his mission, his destiny's call.
He cares not for the safety and security on the way,
No matter how arduous the climb is,
How dangerous the path is, he must dare.

He is drawn by that which is beyond him,
He is sustained by a fire that he is yet to find;
And he knows in the very depths of his heart that
He is a son of fire and
This knowledge sustains him in his solitude.
Into the fire, he goes like a moth offering himself.

~

Let the fire be,
Let the blazing strength of fire find its way,
Let the flaming tongues of fire take delight in you,
Let the fire be free and radiant in your words and gaze.

~

Be the Fire.

~

I have no army
Or an armour.
I will come alone
Even if it is war.

~

When Rudra's breath is stirring your depths,
When his fire is ready to burst forth,
Behold and let go of all your coverings.
Come out in the fields and explode
Like a long-awaited volcanic eruption.
God is not only the dewdrops and the moonshine,
He is also the thunder and the lightning fire.

~

When truth burns you
Allow the flame to consume you utterly.
Cry not to spare you
For once Shiva cast his eyes upon you,
Be ready to die in the naked blaze of truth.

~

When the fire is roaring in you,
Know that your walls are crumbling.
When the great God is released,
Yes, there comes destruction,
The destruction of all that is holding
You back from what you truly are.

~

Let the fire be;
Adorations to the one
Whom the ancients knew.

Merciless is the hands of your potter,
Behold thy clay in willing servitude
For the artist fingers to mould you
To perfection and adorn your body
With flame-kissed patterns of delight.

~

In the naked blaze of truth, burn;
Burn to the extent of invincible might,
Burn to the truth of utterly blazing light,
To the sun's fiery embrace,
To the summer's desert vastness,
To the lone climber's Everest summit.

And be alone, fearless in your truth
Uncontaminated in golden purity.

~

A fire-born heart remains always golden,
Noble and precious, free from all stains.

~

Technology begins and ends with Agni
The great fire;
And all fires lead to the Dawn,
The Supreme Goddess, the mother of all fires.

~

Luminous intensity is a gift of fire.
That which is asleep in seed and strives in the plant
When it awakens in you, know that you must find the sun,
The fullness of your blazing brilliance.

~

The fire that lights the suns, the fire that leaps through the lightning, the fire that burns at the kernel of earth, the fire that bursts forth as volcanoes – it is the same fire that is tamed and yoked as hunger that drives living creatures. Life-devouring life, the fire climbs towards the mating drive and endless cravings of desire that pushes the boundaries to expand and enlarge one's possessions; to build territories and empires, to possess more and more land and resources, more and more money and power, to assert and command the world. The fire-will to conquer is infinite and the war and conquest unquenched drives man towards infinity through violence and fury of fire's infinite hunger.

Then it touches the mind and becomes the quest for knowledge; the fire gets calmer and becomes illuminations and the dawning of knowledge. The quest for knowledge and empires of knowledge breaks down all forms of the past knowing and constantly recreate and rebuild knowledge towards greater perfection, towards all knowledge; the call of infinity demands convergence and synthesis, a vision of the whole, the totality of existence. Only in that wholesome vision of knowledge, wisdom is born and blooms as love and delight, harmony and beauty in the experience of Oneness. The splendours of light and delight burst forth as Nature's bridal beauty of spring. Then the sun and earth are married in man and he discovers honeycombs growing full in his heart, the golden fire of delight, the nectar of Love's splendour.

Then alone is a man ready for the festival of gods on earth.

~

If a sense of incompletion, imperfection and that strange feeling of missing something is not haunting us, we are yet to be human.

To be discontent is a unique human privilege.

To be driven by a fire within that won't allow us to remain content in our daily routines is the very essence of our human nature.

Animals are not haunted by this discontent; they are happy and whole in their orbits set by Nature and cannot move out of their groves.

But for the man, this very grove becomes a prison he rebels against, the fire within demands him to leave behind the known and dare the abyss.

That is what makes us creative; our creativity sets us apart from the animals, a fire that burns through us creating and destroying at the same time.

On the trails of this fire, is set man's destiny.

No artist can remain content with his latest creation; he is always called by a greater call, a greater impulsion, seeking expression.

Every peak he climbs reveals always new peaks of splendour that he cannot resist.

~

If you have not dealt with the fire in you,
The fire will burn you down.
You may repress it, you may run away from it
But nothing is going to help you.

You must face the wrath of fire
That has never found its expression;
The wrath of Rudra, the merciless
Compassion of the thundering might.

To give flaming intensities
To his invigorating strength is to know him
Intimately as you know yourself;
And to break free from the chains of fear
And express your truth as it is
With its naked strength no matter what it is.

You have been told of the devil in you,
The sinner, the traitor and the oppressor,
The animal instincts to be chained
And pushed deep into the cellars of darkness.

So that you can wear the placid exteriors
Of social norms and follow the crowd
Being lead to the shopping malls and voting booths
Where you can enjoy the illusion of choice
And get certified for being good.

But the fire won't spare you when you are left alone
And haunt you with an empty ache
That has no reason or voice but stays within
Till you face and open the lid
Of all that is left unsaid and put on a leash for ages
And let them speak and express
The vast reserves of energy that would set you free.

~

Animals keep away from fire, but it is the privilege of human beings to befriend the fire and make it his guardian. Throughout history, the fire has empowered humanity and has driven the growth of civilisations. While ancients have worshipped the fire, the modern man treats the fire as a slave yoked to do his work, to cook his meals or to go to Mars. Ancient seers had surrendered to the fire and were carried by the fire across many dimensions of existence; whereas the modern man is desperately trying to control it and even in the physical dimension, he is miserably failing. He has become a firefighter as the fire is now raging across the world going wild. It has become the voracious consumer hunger, the very engine of his economy, and it is now burning down his own house playing havoc in the ecosystem. He is yet to learn who the fire is; he doesn't know that the fire is not only an objective phenomenon in Nature but also burns within him upon an ascending scale from hunger to all-embracing love passing through many gradations in between. He is yet to know this divine spark within.

It is the new science emerging in the world, the science of inner fire, a new science that is as ancient as humanity. What the ancient seers knew, the new ones are rediscovering lead by the fire.

To know the fire, you must become the fire.

There is no other way.

~

When you define, you confine;
And in confinement flames the potency of a seed.

~

To be dissatisfied is to be human, that's what makes us different from the rest of the creation. It is the engine behind our creativity; it is the invisible fire that propels us beyond the boundary.

~

Scream not when the flame is upon your very substance, it is the fire of transformation. In your adoration and self-giving, lies the path of least resistance, but remember the infinite has infinite ways of dealing with the finite and always be ready for surprises. The process of awakening is joyful when you know the flame as the embrace of your beloved. Then, then only he pours into you the wine of ecstasy for the gods to feast in the arena of life.

~

Life is where the fire is
Fire is where the heat is
Heat is where the friction is
Friction is where the action is
Action is where the change is
Change is where the will is
Will is where the inspiration is
Inspiration is where the vision is.
Then you are fired up
Then you come alive
Then your respiration and perspiration are worth it.

~

Letting go of expired relationships, however creative they were in the past, is one of the lessons life teaches when you open yourself to the fire of evolutionary growth. You are compressing the journey of many lifetimes into single life. Many people will come your way, spend time with you, be creative together, enjoy, have fun and grow together till it is time for them to depart as if the fire in your relationship is gone and it is time for them to go. To let them go gracefully and consciously is an art worth learning and even more important is to bless them in their new trajectory.

~

When the fire is sweet and gentle
Like fresh honey from flowers
Stay quiet, allowing the flame to reach
The deepest depths of your being
Where a thousand words await
To whisper their treasured secrets.

~

When the fire is soaring high
Upon the wings of imagination
Riding on the winds of delight,
You will see the sunrise
Upon the horizon's brilliant splendours
Painting the glory of life.

~

Concentration gathers scattered energy and directs it towards our chosen goal. That is how we kindle the fire of will, like a lens gathering light to focus so that it can light up and burn things.

~

When the flame is upon you, surrender.
Renounce all your ideas, preferences, attachments
And the fears and the sorrows and the wounds of life
Along with the things you have struggled to change.

There is nowhere to turn but to walk,
Walk straight into the flame even if you tremble.
He is the bridge, the ascending cone of fire,
The bright godhead dear to the seers.

Give utterly all that you are, both good and bad,
Give without reserve, every fibre and cell.
Let his flaming tongues burn you down
Till there is nothing left to cast a shadow.

Know his devouring might and burning will
Know his flaming intensity and mighty focus
Know your body as his warm density
Know your strength as his growing delight.

When there is nothing left but the flame
Know his calm strength in your nerves
Know his luminous gaze and warmth
As if love has a body to dwell.

~

Agni, the flame of aspiration,
The godhead worshipped by the ancient seers
And worshipped by the new.

Deep in the cavern of the heart,
As small as a thumb, dwells the inner guide,
The impeller of our evolutionary progress.

The immortal in the mortals
The knower of all our past births
And the course of our present birth.

Salutations, O' Fire.

~

Chapter 4

Aspiration

Our longing is to belong forever and yet
We are vagabonds, uprooted, wandering nomads.
Our identities are crumbling and new ones are fleeting.
We are a ferment yet to grow wings.
We have lost our moorings and we have reached nowhere.
We still cling to our familiar bonds,
Hoping for light in a world that is falling apart,
A world that has become a ferment in itself.
We are forever in a transit lounge,
Waiting for a flight that has no number or destination.

~

When my heart starts singing, I would know.
Till then it is only searching and seeking
Longing and in despair like a fish out of water.
Life in the water was good and safe
Like a baby in a womb
To come out is to breathe differently
And to learn to cry out for help;
And the help comes, always.

Out of all the noises of the world,
You would hear a lullaby
One song stands out, one voice soft and sweet
She is the golden bridge, the wonderful fire.

~

Habit > Craving > Desire > Drive > Passion > Will >
Longing > Aspiration > Home

Browse your way back home.

~

Inspirations sweep in as a response to our aspirations.
It is the universe breathing into us giving aha moments of
revelations and dynamic power of action.

~

If aspiration is a latent force, inspiration is its living dynamic power in action.

~

I love the mountains, their stillness and majesty, their peaks and valleys, their rich forests and the scary wildlife. Staying in a cottage somewhere in the Western Ghats, I see these mountain ranges in front. The sense of the sacred feels natural here. Mother nature with all her glory and mystic depths. Sitting in her lap like a little child and wondering how I am to know her. I can hear the wild birds, the sound of nearby waterfalls, the crickets and the innumerable instruments of her symphony of life. I breathe fresh air and feel the joy in my body. Isn't it amazing that this little human body is an integral part of her body and being and yet I feel so separate from her? I am a prisoner of my own mind and its thoughts. The relentless flow of thoughts cuts me off from the mystery of one body and one life that thrives as Nature. When I look behind thoughts, into the silence, and reach out to her body through my inner senses, it feels like immersing in an ocean of energy. Her embrace is rejuvenating and intoxicating. She heals as if it is the most natural process, Nature restores the harmony and the breath deepens with gratitude. I feel like a drop longing to merge back into the ocean of her being.

~

A seed can remain as a seed for a very long time till it is touched by the awakening grace of rain and sunshine. Till then it is in a sleep state, the potential is there but waiting for the right conditions. So are we, potentially divine, but actually in sleep. Our divine nature is only a potentiality, not an actuality. Then comes the call for the adventure and when the call reaches the soul, something in us awakens, but the mind has no clue and it has to figure things out through a period of trial and error. The more we listen to the depths of our heart, our natural longing towards a greater beauty, harmony, truth, goodness, freedom and delight grows in strength and eventually reveals itself as a longing to unite with the divine.

This longing is the flame of our aspiration. This aspiration is not will or intention, though will can support the movement of aspiration. Nor is it desire or craving.

This aspiration in its early stage is veiled and there is a growing longing in the heart for something that the mind has no words to explain. However, a seemingly random sequence of events would take you forward and the path reveals itself as you start walking following your intuition. Slowly you would discover that there is a living response, a Presence and Grace guiding you and leading your way. Once you become conscious of this Grace, the path becomes more and more sunlit and joyful. There is less and less effort, more and more surrender and sadhana become a graceful flow of sweet gladness as the divine Mother reveals increasingly her ocean of love in which you exist.

~

The call is always there surrounding us like an invisible presence, nudging us to come out of the comfort zone and explore the vast. Its rays are often finding ways to awaken our soul and the depths are often stirred. Yet the moments fade off, we are too busy with our laundry list. There is never enough time; we are forever waiting for that ideal day when there is enough time. We have sold our precious time in the marketplace to earn some money, reluctantly. We do our daily chores half-heartedly, our self-giving feels incomplete, empty of the juice of delight.

~

There is no one to blame even if it is convenient to blame a politician or businessman out there. It is not the fault of our kith and kin and no one has the key to open the doors of light within us. Each one of us has to do it ourselves, by listening deeply to our longings, to have the courage to accept it and allow it to burn us down completely, all our pretensions must go. There is no other way, the flame of radiance demands our surrender, complete self-giving.

~

There is a gentle form of sadness with which our soul communicates to our outer consciousness. When we deny what our soul is longing for, when we go against its call, instead of demanding and pushing, the soul withdraws. Then we feel deep in the heart this gentle quiet sadness standing back without engaging in our outer activities.

Often our daily schedules and demands of life are so completely occupying we do not even get time to pay attention to this gentle sadness within. Or even when we feel its presence, we wrap it up in one or other rational explanations and brush it aside.

The more we deny the call of our soul, the more we neglect this message of sadness from the soul, the more distant it becomes and eventually gets veiled by the noise of our mind. Over a period, numbness sets in and we lose our ability to feel as we build a barrier against it. All that is left is the cold rationalizations and increasing tension within as we get harder with ourselves or distract or drown ourselves in external entertainments, addictions or consumerist objects of desire.

The search for happiness takes on more and more need for the dramatic intensity of external experiences as it is the only way to get across the numbness that has set in. The more the wall of numbness thickens between the soul and the outer personality, the more strange ways the soul finds to break down the wall. Tragedies, failures and depressions, strange attractions towards the taboo, the illegitimate, the mysterious and streaks of strange behaviour that erupt into the normalcy of daily routines are some of the ways by which the soul creates conditions that break down the inner wall of separation.

Passing through such a turbulent period in life is often described as the dark night of the soul; it is a passage through the darkness towards the dawning of the soul. The more we pay attention to the inner discomfort and follow its trails, the less the need for turbulence and painful experiences. By paying attention to the inner gentle reminders, we learn the language of the soul and the more we listen, the more the soul reveals. As the link with our inmost light strengthens, the flowering of the soul takes on a course of movement from light to greater light, joy to greater joy. Our outer life may go through dramatic shifts that may appear to be chaotic, but inwardly we grow more and more luminous and harmonious.

~

Chapter 5

Grace

Your gracefulness is an expression of your soulfulness.

~

If Karma is logic, Grace is magic.

~

Where there is self-giving, unconditional self-giving, there is also the grace of radiance. When there is no doubt, when there is no fear, when there is no demand, then the self-giving is complete and there is the sheer joy of giving; then there is the fragrance of the soul in our self-giving. Then opens the space for grace to flow in and our soul comes alive.

~

The trouble is we do not know how to give ourselves; we are unsure, we are scared or we are trading with life, being clever, trying to get some returns, making a strategic investment when we give. Such self-giving is weak and incapable of opening the doors of grace.

~

Your ignorance of the divine grace doesn't prove its non-existence.

~

When you are open to grace, your life will become
graceful. You will see all that is happening in your life as
an act of grace. Even the most painful events will reveal
themselves to be an act of grace taking you beyond your
imagination. Once you see a greater Wisdom guiding your
life, surrender will become natural and easy. Then your
life will start flowing gracefully and effortlessly.

~

Yesterday while roaming around in a busy street a stranger came in front me showing a bunch of keys. It took me a few seconds to notice that it was my bunch of keys! I was surprised as I had not even noticed them falling off my pocket. I thanked him quickly and received the keys. It was very easy to brush aside the incident as pure chance, nothing significant and forget about it considering it as just luck and chance. But the more I look for the divine the more I see the Presence and constant protection. The minute care is such even in my unconsciousness there is always this grace acting. If I had lost my keys it would have been such difficulty but the divine love saw to it that I was protected just in time.

When I shared this to my friend she said "Wonderful, however, please don't take it as a license to be unconscious!" So true!

It was like another loving message from the divine.

I felt gratitude welling up within me.

It happened right after I shared a photo yesterday - "key to happiness..." as if the lesson was planned in advance.

The more you see the action of grace the more gratitude you experience.

~

Career by chance

Life is unfolding in a haphazard manner by chance and you do whatever comes on your way. Some work you love, some you hate. But still, there are rays of hope and aha moments occasionally and you are always hoping for miracles to happen.

Career by choice

When you are fed up with doing boring stuff, you master courage and go after what you love doing, find your passion and direct your life the way you want it to unfold. You have a dream, you have a passion, you have a vision and you have the drive to make it happen. You do what you deeply love doing.

Career by grace

You discover that what seems to be done by your personal choice and will is actually coming from a greater Presence and Power. You develop deep humility and gratitude and wonder what is in store for you, what is the Will of that Presence guiding and moulding you into. You surrender to That and love all that is coming on your way as nothing but that grace in action. You come in touch with That and fall in love with that Mystery, the mystery of the One who is moulding you. Then you get drunk in love and all that you do become the radiance of that love.

~

"If you want to know the Divine Grace, take up some work that inspires you but is far beyond your capacity!" said one of my friends during breakfast. He was not giving me any theoretical knowledge; I have seen him manifesting some major projects in Auroville starting without any money or people or even knowledge of how to do it, but he has always managed to realise his dreams. He said "when you take up these big dreams you will be always in difficulty and always praying for help and the help comes, miracles happen and things get done. You can see that it is the divine grace doing everything, you are only an instrument." It felt so true.

First of all, we believe that we are in charge of managing our life and work and the capacity for doing it is entirely ours. It is so satisfying for our ego, the very idea of a greater power overseeing our life and work is very difficult to conceive and experience, especially when we are doing the daily round of small things. But when inspiration takes us to domains that are far beyond what one can imagine, then our eyes begin to open to see the presence of a greater intelligence organising, governing the unfolding of the course of our life and work.

~

Healing and normalising sexual energy is a long journey; most of us grow up wounded by life one way or another. There is a wounded child within an adult and is behind the veil of every depression or aggression. It is only when we come in touch with this child and explore deeper that we learn that is not limited to our personal journey, it goes through our parents to our family context through generations and the general social context in which each one of us has been brought up. Our responses to life situations are so much governed by these undercurrents and we are seldom aware of its uneasy presence. That makes the healing process cyclic as the deeper layers show up with growing awareness, to be cleansed and energies liberated. What starts off as an individual journey opens into a collective journey and therefore long and difficult. Yet with the river of grace, the horse stable can be cleansed as Hercules did. The river of grace, Ganga, flows down from above into the darker layers of our being purifying and liberating centuries of pain and suffering.

~

Truth is a pathless land, said J.Krishnamurti. When I read it for the first time, I was puzzled and fascinated but I couldn't grasp its meaning. There was something in it and yet beyond my reach. It was he who knocked me out of slumber. I realised that I was on a highway, among a crowd following a well laid mainstream life. Then I turned into less travelled country roads and that was far more enjoyable. Unlike the highway where I could hear only the sound of others honking, on the country roads I could hear my own thoughts. Then I took further turns into solitary thin trails through the forests and mountains where I could even hear my heartbeats. There I met rare pilgrims and the silent presence and grace of the masters who walked these solitary trails. After that even the thin trails disappeared, there was no more any path, you are all alone in a vast expanse. There were no more thoughts and ideas to cling to. You are face to face with primal ignorance, and all knowledge vanishes seeing the futility of it in the face of the surrounding immensity. There is no system that can help. You are walking all alone, with a silent mind, breathing fresh air in wonderment facing the mysterious universe, in the lap of the unknowable.

All that is left is Grace and a nameless Presence, that makes you take the right steps at the right time.

Then the words of JK came back and made sense, truth is a pathless land.

~

Guru is not a teacher
Or a domain expert;
Guru is a presence
A field in which
The doors to grace
Are wide open.

~

Chapter 6

Surrender

Ego bargains,
Soul gives joyfully.

~

I am scared of your love's longing depths.
Like an ocean tide, your presence builds up
And I hold onto my safe shores
Unwilling to let go of my little self.

~

The joy of self-giving, the joy of surrender, is a privilege of the soul.

Every other part of our being tremble, resist, fear, calculate, doubt or even revolt against a complete self-giving and surrender. Only the soul has the certitude of love and the radiance of utter self-giving.

This makes the way of the soul sunlit and delightful.

~

Learn to give yourself, not just your petty coins and toys.

~

Wherever there is self-giving, unconditional self-giving,
love is bound to manifest.
Love and self-giving are two sides of the same movement.
Love never asks "What will I get?"
Love's question is "What can I give?"
Only in love's radiance giving is joyful.
Only in love's abundance, self-giving is supremely
expansive and nourishing.
Only in love's delight self-giving is effortless and graceful.
Therefore fear not, ever, to give yourself when love's joy is
upon your heart.

~

Ego not only has its view but also its boundary.
As the ego gets harder, so does its view and its boundary.
It is a developmental stage, to mentally individualize.

But to get stuck there is to eventually suffocate in
one's own exaggerated self-importance and false self.
Surrendering this ego requires conscious effort, an effort to
listen to the deeper intuition and to follow its call.

~

When love dawns upon you, ego surrenders gladly.
As your self-giving deepens, love becomes profound
adoration.
In adoration, you discover the sacred, and the sacred
naturally brings worship.
Worship is the way of the soul illumined by the splendour
of the Beloved.

~

The trouble with love is that it churns our depths ruthlessly till we surrender completely. Love is meticulous when it comes to demanding our perfection and harmony. Till every fibre of our being is purified and surrendered the churning continues and the ego screams all the way while getting dragged to be in the presence of the Sacred.

~

When the wind blows over the leaves, only the ripe and ready leaves let go off from the branch and fly off surrendering to the wind. What truly matters is not the wind but the readiness of the leaves, the wind is only an occasion.

So are all the techniques we use to transform ourselves; hundreds may use the same technique but only a few make some real change. It is not so much the technique, the technique or practice is only an occasion, what truly matters is our readiness to let go and surrender.

~

One of the great dangers on the way is when the individual ego crystallises.

When we start the journey the ego itself is not sufficiently formed, we are still part of the collective ego. As we proceed on the path, leaving behind the well-trodden highways and its second-hand knowledge, we will eventually find our solitary trails and discover our own experiential knowledge. Such discovery brings its exhilaration and resultant confidence, a confidence that builds our individual ego and its capacity to stand on its own against a world that seems to more and more like an unconscious crowd of automation.

Besides, when our individual trail brings worldly recognition and success, the ego gets further reinforced in its own certitudes and declares its own freedom and asserts itself. That's when the crystallisation of the ego in its own world view begins to harden and you get encrusted in your own self-created jail. Eventually, it becomes quite lonely out there inside the shell.

You have not yet found your soul, you have only formed an individual ego. It gets worse when you have worldly success and a public image to protect as it has become your identity. Many people linger there unwilling to go further. While it is part of the process to mentally individualise but this is still a mental ego, not yet the true person, the soul within.

But now you are ready to surrender, you have built something that can be surrendered, offered, dissolved so that a greater light can dawn upon you replacing the surface personality.

~

There is nothing as calming and settling like finding your master, the master of your soul. It is not a choice that your mind can make, it is made for you by your soul. Your mind may still remain ignorant but once the choice is made deep within, your wanderings would come to an end. Increasingly you would find yourself drawn to a magnet you can no more ignore, someone strangely becomes the centre of your life and you return again and again to that source as if your soul is getting nourished every time you return. Something in you has already surrendered, given itself utterly and the rest of your parts are still figuring out what is happening. One by one they too will open up and surrender to the guiding light, but it takes time. But the fundamental difficulty is over once you recognise the presence of the master within.

~

The very events that set in motion your awakening are often experienced as causing a great deal of pain; but that which is getting hurt, that which is suffering is actually the ego, your wall of resistance. Behind this wall dwells the divinity within you, untouched, pure and calm rejoicing in the touch of the infinite. But you are not in touch with this flame of delight within while the events are unfolding and hence the experience of pain and suffering.

While the ego is dreading surrender our soul has already surrendered. As long as you remain identified with your ego, your surface personality, your petty little ideas about yourself, your emotional attachments, needs and habits, the suffering continues.

It is the ego that suffers.
It is the ego that feels lonely.
It is the ego that feels terrified.
It is the ego that feels betrayed.
It is the ego that feels as separate.

The soul knows no boundaries; it gives itself entirely in a cry of adoration.

The only way to end your suffering is to go beyond the surface personality into the very depths of your being where dwells the calm flame of your true being who knows the alchemist orchestrating the events unfolding in your life. It is this flame within that knows the mighty embrace of the infinite and let the hands of the infinite crush and mould you to perfection. It is this flame within that knows the splendour of the Beloved. But to adore and surrender you must know the One behind all masks.

~

If you have not known the love of the infinite how can you ever love the infinite?

But to know the love of the infinite you must go beyond all forms and see the infinite hands of the mighty potter shaping your clay to perfection. Once your heart is smitten you cannot escape any more, for the infinite embraces you from all sides; as an enemy as well as the beloved giving you no doors to escape - for he has chosen you towards a greater destiny.

Your stiffness is mellowed by waters of gentle affection and once you are pliable enough you are pounded mercilessly till your very substance yields to the gentlest of his suggestions. Then you are put on the wheel of life and spun into forms that reveal his pleasant imaginations and always be ready for a surprise as you can be anything that you have never dreamt of before.

When you are surprised by your own new birth you are put into the fire along with his other creations to burn into you new strength and bring out the colours of your unique splendour. Scream not when the flame is upon your very substance, it is the fire of transformation.

In your adoration and self-giving lies the path of least resistance, but remember the infinite has infinite ways of dealing with the finite and always be ready for the surprise. The process of awakening is joyful when you know the flame as the embrace of your beloved.

Then, then only he pours into you the wine of ecstasy for the gods to feast in the arena of life.

~

A time comes in your journey when you are done with all the external conversations and investigations. All the answers you sought now you know lies within and you have no choice but to turn your gaze inward.

There is nowhere to go, no teachers, no books, no destinations outside. You are left with your inner world and its endless landscapes and a thousand voices.

Somewhere in that a faint or occasionally clear inner voice guides your steps.

There's a reversal, the outer world makes sense only in terms of the inner and many things you thought were near and dear turn out to be far and strange.

A solitude envelope you and all are now strangers or faces once loved but no more the same, familiar and yet unfamiliar. All that you hold dear as knowledge falls apart as useless and the humming sound in your cranium becomes just another noise, a thought crunching machine parsing words like a hungry dog chewing bones.

Can you please stop that machine?

It makes no sense any more, the labour of the thinker.

There are two ways to step out of the machine, one is into the empty void beyond words and the other is into the very substance of your body and it's vibrant energy.

If you take the path of emptiness you extinguish and there is nothing but a void that has no purpose in particular except to run the course of its bodily life and dissolve the physical existence in time.

But if you take the path of the body you become a traveller of the worlds. The thick crust of matter thins out to be a veil guarding many mysteries. Behind the same face, you meet many people or behind many faces, you meet the same person. You are no more relating in the same way, your reality and all the meanings that made sense are getting reformatted.

Then you look at yourself and wonder who is this fellow, the stranger inside you, the many people and their voices inside you, the ripples of joy and the undercurrents of sorrow – all that belongs to an impersonal substratum in which the body is moving.

When the identities fail to make sense you know that you have become a nomad, you have no address and destination. All you have is an inner call like the pole star, everything else is just signs pointing your way. And you don't know where you are going... But you know, you must explore and go where it takes you.

~

Your inner strength is directly proportional to your surrender to that which is carrying you forward.

~

Leave aside your scientific contraptions and the ego outside the temple wall.

You can enter the soul space only through love, adoration, worship and surrender.

~

There is a magnet out there, a call, secretly drawing you towards it, gently and mysteriously.

You may call it God, Guru, Ideal, Purpose, Vision, Dream or whatever label you are comfortable with. The label is irrelevant, what matters is your recognition that you are being drawn towards a mystery that gets deeper and fascinating the more you explore it.

Initially, the process is confusing, slow and chaotic as you stumble your way through life and the signals seem to be random. But later the signals become more coherent and you start reading into the future, into a glory you can't really grasp.

At one point you know that your life has meaning and joy only with respect to that call and everything else becomes secondary. Even all the people around you make less and less sense when you realise that you are listening to another song, a song that is unique to you.

It takes courage to leave behind the known and follow the call, then you are on your own, coming in terms with your solitude. Only strength you have is the faith in the call and your complete surrender.

You would feel safe enough to dissolve yourself.

Then something will take birth in you, a new being.

A being who is quiet and glad, fresh like morning dew and wide as the dawn.

~

Chapter 7

Love

Your soul has only one secret to deliver - Love.

~

When love's depth runs deeper than words
Your whole being is a prayer for the beloved.

~

Beloved is a multitude!

~

It has rained.
The summer had been long, very long.
Awake at night I was listening
As if you have not spoken for ages.

~

When people talk about love, they talk about relationships.
What if the reality is an ocean of Love?
What if our longing for love is a call from the Source?
What if the very act of breathing is an act of love?
Can we then sit alone and enjoy in our solitude,
The ocean of love that permeates all things?

~

Love makes your face glow and your eyes radiant.
To be radiant is to be in touch with your soul.
Your mind is only an instrument of expression,
A means to give form to your inner joy.
When you use your mind to find this joy,
You are putting the cart in front of the horse.
Be seated in the heart and let the mind follow the radiance.
But beware, your heart is an ocean;
Deep in the ocean are the pearls of radiance,
whispers of delight shut in the shells of solitude.

~

I am the fall and the glory
I am the sinner and the saint
I am the night and the day.
In me are the extremes,
The most impossible extremes
That would never unite
And yet, I behold them both
The two ends of my being
As one in the eternity of love.

~

Narrow hearts will be crushed open,
So a wider love can enter and dwell.
It may hurt, but the beloved is ruthless
When it comes to claiming
A wider space within you.

~

Love for knowledge cannot rest
Until it becomes the knowledge of love.
Love for power cannot rest
Until it becomes the power of love.
In love, both knowledge and power
Come home and rejoice.

~

Love for knowledge is great, but the knowledge of what?

~

When you start missing someone you have never found,
know that you are ready for a greater love.

~

Loving someone or something is only a beginning
The goal is to become love itself.

~

Love is not a person out there,
It is the very fragrance of your own soul.

~

For the untrained eyes, a lover and a madman look almost
the same. Waiting for the Beloved, the one and the only
one is a sublime emotion.

If the Presence is a splendour of adoration, seconds are
eternities doorways. Those who know, know and those who
do not, do not; says the wise.

So are you and me, two sides of one reality, surrendering to
each other In a flow of attractions, over the rims of danger-
pools of non-existence.

To love you as you are is to love me as I am; so be it, says
the mystery. It is a new dawn, your smile, upon the earth
and I wish to be lost in your splendour.

~

How does one distinguish between the movements of love, desire and attachment? They come mixed up and it is a great challenge to distinguish the gold from its fake imitations.

In love, there is joyous self-giving, adoration, expansion, harmony, effortless creativity, radiance, freedom, sense of wholeness, peace and delight.

In desire, instead of self-giving there is pulling of the object of desire towards oneself, craving, contraction, tension, anxiety, impatience, restlessness and sense of incompletion.

In attachment, there is pulling of the object of love towards oneself, fear of losing, dependency, bondage, possessiveness, limitation and the sense of incompletion.

When there is a glimpse of love immediately comes the desire and attachment that covers it up and extinguishes it in the process. It takes some practice to segregate these movements.

The greatest joy is to discover that love does not depend on any external objects or conditions, but it is a radiant state of our own inmost being.

Desire and attachment are always tied to some external objects or conditions.

~

Love never demands, love always gives.

When you say "you don't love me", you are not experiencing yourself from the radiant source of your own being; instead you are identified with the surface ego-self having its boundary shut off from your own soul of love.

So you complain "you don't love me", no matter to whom the complaint goes it is an inner condition.

But when your ego opens the doors and lets the light of your love radiate from your heart, then you have the experience "I love you", no matter to whom the radiance goes.

~

Love, who wants to resist it?

But the fact is, most do.

Love is the most frightening thing for an adult ego, it must sacrifice itself and that is not a price everyone is willing to pay.

~

Want to awaken?

The easiest and fastest way is to fall in love, but don't ask me how!

Love has no techniques, schedules and timelines; you can't fix an appointment for that. The point is, it is not about your 'doing' anything in particular.

Allow your heart to be stolen.

~

With love comes death, the death of our ego, the false self
of separation;
Hence the pain, the burns and the misery of love born from
the desire to possess.
To know the flame is to offer yourself like a moth and
become the flame.

~

Love is a natural fragrance of your soul.
It has nothing much to do with someone out there.
And yet the presence of someone out there may burst open
the lotus of your heart.
You may long to pour out your love.
You may feel deeply vulnerable fearing the rejection of
your love.
Or if you are lucky you may find that space between you
two to be a perfect place for a sweetness you cannot fully
grasp.
And yet when you claim the other you start building the
walls that would eventually turn your inner landscape
barren.
This fiery sweet love cannot live in narrow confines of
human attachments and possessiveness.
It would die of suffocation if it is to be bound.
Love is boundless, only in a vaster sky, your love can
spread wings.

~

If a woman is to heal her relationship with the man she has to come in terms with her role in creating him. He cannot be what he is without her creative power, without her empowering him to be what she imagines him to be. The day the woman discovers her creative power generating him, that will be the day of her freedom.

She is yet to know the man as her own creation and the sole power is within her to mould him.

~

Friends are my memory of love.
Older the love more precious it is;
It is like wine, getting better with time;
Some new ones are as ancient as the dawn.

~

Nearness has nothing much to do with physical distance, it
is all about dearness.

~

Knowledge, Will and Love are the triple keys to open the secrets of life.

Knowledge shows the way, Will carries you forward and Love is the destination.

The knowledge becoming force is the Will and the harmonious union of many wills gives the experience of Love. They are three facets of one movement.

To be in love is to experience the glad flowering of harmony.

~

Once a professor, from Jerusalem University, asked me "Why limit yourself to Sri Aurobindo? Why don't you read other masters? There are so many wonderful teachers out there."

I had a good laugh, I told him "Look, it is like falling in love, once you fall for your beloved you won't search anymore, you have come home."

It amuses me often when people directly or indirectly suggest I open up and read wide and become more knowledgeable about the various teachings. Otherwise, you are seen as somewhat narrow and rigid. Usually, such suggestions come from people who have some aversion towards Gurus and imagine themselves to be liberal and independent.

They miss the point that it is not really about knowledge, it is the mystery of love.

It is a blessing when you find your heart at home with someone beyond any trace of doubt.

That's what centres you, that's what anchors you.

The rest are details of your unfolding in the presence of your beloved.

~

Eyes are for scientists an organ with anatomy, biology, chemistry, physics etc

But for an artist, poet or a lover, eyes are the doorways to a world of wonder;

It is that wonder that matters - that elusive something that is utterly real.

~

When your words are flowing, know that I am with you.
When you are in full bloom, know that my love is
blooming in you.
When you are awake know that I am looking through you.

~

When all things are said and done
What remains is the heart speak
The hushed tone of secret words
Things I did not speak, the love
I am yet to find a way to express
The sweetness you are to me.

~

If pain hasn't pierced deep into your heart
What would you know about your own depths?
In your self-giving is the heart of intimacy
And the nourishing groves of the sacred garden.
When the gods find your treasures bloom
Storms are sent to uproot your safe havens.
Then your bleeding depths are left open wide
In the night for the stars to chant their anthem
Of greater mercy and wider love's harmony
Awakening you to a glad tide of infinity.

~

To know the Woman is to know Love.
She is a temple where love is worshipped.
If you are a beggar, sit outside the temple walls and beg.
If you are a trader, sell flowers and incense on the streets to the temple.
If you are a devotee, enter the temple to worship and be in awe of her architecture of infinite splendour.
If you are a priest of love, your work is worship in her temple of eternity.
And if you are Love, know yourself as her Beloved, the deity, and enjoy the rhythms of her heartbeat creating the worlds.

~

Relax into my being
Into my stillness
Where we meet
On this bridge
Of words
Where we gaze
Upon each other.

Here, we meet,
Right now
As your breath
As your heartbeat
As your beloved eyes,
Let me be your smile.
Allow me to kiss you
Quietly from inside.

~

The Master is invisible
Till the heart is sunny
And the eyes are well lit.

~

I do not know
Where I end
Or you begin
Or whether
I am looking for you
Or you are looking for me.
We are two sides
Of the same person
Strangely divided.

~

Drop your thoughts
And be a seer
Nay, be my lover
Then you shall know
My ways, quiet and sweet,
A million rays
Cast in stillness.
Then you shall smile
As dawn itself
In a quiet splendour.

~

My pilgrimage Towards your temple
Is a series of confessions
Of all my forceful deeds
To assert my will
Against your ways.

Now, as I kneel down
With a prayer in my heart,
I wonder why you have
Allowed all that
In the first place.

Strange are your ways
To even let me crumble
In shame and guilt
Or let me wander
Lost in confusions.

And yet your smile comes
When I am about to give up.
I wonder why
You have given me
All this freedom
To explore your depths
In many strange ways
That I cannot fathom.

Maybe there is a reason;
Without this freedom
How can I ever know
The nature of your infinite love
That never demands anything
And yet gives everything
As if you have been
Always waiting
For me to come back.

~

As long as the enemy is your focus
You will remain a sword in this world.
Speak not of peace with your sharp edges
In supreme tenderness does love kisseth.

~

Whenever I have
Leapt over
To possess you,
To own you,
To make you mine
You have flowed
Through my hands
And faded away,
Like morning mist.

Dear one,
Now I am afraid
To claim you as mine
Or to break my still gaze
As you come back
And settle quietly
In my garden.

~

Your smile is complete in itself
I have come home all alone
Nowhere to go, nothing to do
Just be in your depths
Watching sunrise hues.

~

As you are near, very near,
In the stillness of my being
I want to be quiet, very quiet;
So that I can feel your smile
In every cell of my body.

~

I can hide in your words
Play with your lips
Gaze into your heart
And see through your secret love.

I can hide in your depths
Swing with your breath
Drum up your heartbeat
And kiss your dreams.

~

Let the breeze tell you
Of the flowers nearby;
The garlands are real.

~

Allow me to tell you this
I see through your eyes
From inside and outside.

~

When your breath is an offering
Every ascent and descent is worship.
In that calm rhythm is your body
Preparing itself for the infinite
For the ever-present mystery of love.

~

Chapter 8

Purpose

In the beginning is concealed the end, like in a seed.

~

Your purpose illumines your path.

~

Purpose kindles motivation.

~

Purposeful action is meaningful action,
Rich in emotions and effortless in the will.

~

From purpose comes the meaning
From meaning comes the emotion
From emotion comes the will
From will comes the action.

~

Purpose > Meaning > Emotion > Will > Action
It is one creative flow, all yoked into each other.

~

What is your purpose?
Purpose of this moment
Purpose of coming one hour
Purpose of the day
Purpose of the week
Purpose of the month
Purpose of the year
Purpose of your life.
The further you see,
The greater the richness
Of this moment's meaning.

~

Our true calling is veiled behind many layers of thoughts, emotions and works we do for all kinds of reasons and that makes it hard to know one's true passion, true calling, true intensity and the joy of doing what one is truly meant to do.

When we do not really know our true calling we go on clinging to all things that are not essential and this clinging perpetuates the veil and covers up our true passion. We justify this clinging by saying "I will stop doing all this once I know what I am really meant to do".

But the fact is what we are truly meant to do cannot reveal or arise till we drop all the junk, all the coverings, all the non-essential things, we go on doing. What we need is courage, great courage and faith, to drop all the non-essential stuff and face the unknown and be comfortable with it.

Then there is space for Grace to flow in and show us the way.

~

It is not your thoughts, the universe is thinking through
you.
It is not your imaginations, the universe is imaging through
you.
It is not your emotions, the universe is emoting through
you.
It is not your actions, the universe is acting through you.

Once you know and see this simple fact and learn to trust
the universe and surrender to its process, you are ready
to discover your purpose. Open to the universe to flow
through you freely. Instead of receiving in droplets, receive
the universe as a stream. Become a flute through which the
universe can flow through as thoughts, as imaginations, as
emotions and as actions.

Then you can see that these thoughts, imaginations, emotions
and actions acquire a new flavour, a new freshness and
originality beyond your normal state. It makes you creative
because the Source is always creative; it is not your creativity,
it is the creativity of your source. This not only makes you
refreshingly original but also joyful and energised and
makes your journey effortless. In that surrender is revealed
your purpose and its inspiring vision.

~

There is an unconscious and mechanical will in a habit;

There is a will of desire, and impulse-driven will that troubles you in shopping malls, that comes and goes in waves;

There is an intense will of passion and heroism that you enjoy during adventures or battles;

There is a will in emotions, love's vulnerable demands;

There is a will of reason, built on logic;

There is a will arising from knowledge, a calmer steady will of pure intelligence and vision;

There is a greater will than all these lesser wills, the Will of your soul you are yet known but is guiding your destiny.

To align with this greater will is to align with your life's purpose and it is this Will that harmonises everything and makes your actions effortless.

~

If you believe yourself to be a victim, the reality
reconfigures itself to be your tyrant.
If you believe yourself to be a warrior, the reality
reconfigures itself to be your opponent.
If you believe yourself to be a lover, the reality
reconfigures itself to be your beloved.
As you seek so you find.
The choice is yours; each role has its rasa, its delight.

~

The more clearly you see your purpose the more alive you become.

~

When you have a vision, you have a purpose;
When you have a purpose, you have the drive;
When you have the drive, you start living;
Then you come alive.

~

It is never too late, not even death can stop you from fulfilling your purpose; you will always come back with a bang!

~

When you do not know what to do, be just that utterly and completely - a pure state of not knowing. Dive deep into its depths till you come in touch with a wave of becoming that will carry you forward. Ride on its crest and enjoy the wonders of a greater self unfolding through you.

~

I keep coming across people who are in transition.

Something beyond them has stepped into their lives and the events are unfolding in such a way they are getting uprooted from their old self. The new self is not yet formed and there is uncertainty and anxiety, but at the same time, there is a deep sense that time has come for an adventure.

I find myself saying, again and again to many people "It is ok not to know, it is time to be comfortable with the state of not knowing. Trust the process."

~

Epilogue

It is the origin and the masterclue,
A silence overhead, an inner voice,
A living image seated in the heart,
An unwalled wideness and a fathomless point,
The truth of all these cryptic shows in Space,
The Real towards which our strivings move,
The secret grandiose meaning of our lives.

- Sri Aurobindo